THE COMPLETE GUIDE TO
CATS AND
DOGS

NICOLA JANE SWINNEY

Sandy Creek
NEW YORK

Sandy Creek
NEW YORK

An Imprint of Sterling Publishing Co., Inc.
1166 Avenue of the Americas
New York, NY 10036

ISBN 978-1-4351-6352-2

Manufactured in China

Lot #:
2 4 6 8 10 9 7 5 3 1
08/16

www.sterlingpublishing.com

CONTENTS

Words in **bold** are explained in the Glossary on page 140.

ALL ABOUT CATS

Cats and people have lived together for at least 12,000 years, since the first farmers began to cultivate cereal crops in the Middle East. Living near humans provided cats with easy hunting, as grain stores attracted mice and rats. Soon cats actively sought human company. People preferred the more friendly types and bred from them, eventually producing today's pampered pets.

The Maine Coon's dappled coat displays its wild heritage. All domestic cats are descended from a wildcat, *Felis sylvestris*.

CATS IN THE WILD

Lions, tigers, leopards, and jaguars are all kinds of **big cat.** Cheetahs belong to their own separate group in the cat family. There are also more than 35 smaller cats, ranging from the muscular cougar to tiny **species** that weigh only a few pounds.

Tigers were once widespread through Asia and southeastern Russia. Today there are fewer than 4,000 left in the wild.

Spotted Cats

Africa's black-footed cat is one of the smallest wildcat species. Its spotty markings, called rosettes, provide perfect **camouflage** in dappled light. It lives in open scrub and grassland, but cats with spotted coats are more often found in forest. The ocelot of North America prefers rainforest and mountains with dense shrub and tree cover. Its range stretches as far north as Arizona and Texas and as far south as Argentina and Uruguay.

Domestic cats share many of the characteristics that make wildcats, such as this ocelot, skilful hunters.

A bobcat's diet is mostly rabbits, mice, and birds, but this hunter will also take down animals much bigger than itself.

Widespread Cat

The lynx is one of the most adaptable wildcats. The North American species, known as the bobcat, is found in swamps, forests, deserts, and even around towns and cities. The Eurasian lynx, which is found across Europe and Asia, is the largest lynx species. A male can top 60 pounds.

FELINE FACTS!

Tigers are the biggest of all wild cat species. An adult male can weigh up to 930 pounds.

CAT COLORS

Some cat breeds only come in certain colors—in others, a whole range of colors and patterns are acceptable.

Colors commonly seen include:

Self or Solid

Each hair on the cat is the same color all the way along.

white

blue

chocolate

lilac

black

White Patches

The cat has areas of white on its coat.

calico

tortoiseshell

Tortoiseshells

A tortoiseshell coat has patches of black, chocolate, or cinnamon over red fur, or patches of blue, lilac, or fawn over cream fur.

Uneven Pigments

If the color on each hair is uneven, the coat doesn't look solidly one color.

Tabby Patterns

A tabby coat has black, brown, silver, or red patterning over paler ticked fur. There are four patterns.

ticked

shaded

smoke

tipped

classic (swirls and blotches)

mackerel (striped)

ears

ticked

mask

nose

spotted

socks

Pointed Coats

The body is paler and the ears, nose, socks, and tail tip are darker.

ANCIENT BREEDS

Many of the older breeds of cat have been used to create the more modern breeds. The Angora, from Ankara in Turkey, is thought to be around 500 years old. All Angoras registered with the **CFA** must have origins that trace back to Turkey.

The Chartreux has rounded, golden eyes that curve upward at the outer corners.

Smiling Feline

Knights returning from the Crusades are said to have introduced the blue-gray Chartreux to French monasteries in the Middle Ages. With its rounded head, sloping forehead, wide cheeks, and narrow **muzzle**, the cat appears to be smiling. The Chartreux is sometimes nicknamed a "potato on toothpicks," because of the skinny legs that support its large body.

FELINE FACTS!

For many years, all long-haired cats were called simply "Angoras."

The Angora is usually thought of as white, but actually comes in more than 20 different colors.

The *mi-ke* (tricolored) Japanese Bobtail is prized by breeders.

Pom-Pom Tail

Japan's native breed of cat, the Japanese Bobtail, is distinguished by its tufted tail. Buddhist monks brought it to Japan during the seventh century CE. Each cat's tail is unique and individual—just like a person's fingerprints. Bobtails can be long- or short-haired and come in all colors.

EXOTICS

Some of the oldest cat breeds come from the East. The Siamese, known for its pointed coat, is from Thailand (once known as Siam). A picture of a pale-coated cat with a dark face, tail, feet, and ears appears in a Thai manuscript from 1350 CE called *The Cat Book Poems*.

BREED PROFILE

NAME: **Siamese**

ORIGIN: **Thailand**

COLORS: **Seal, chocolate, blue, and lilac points**

EYE COLORS: **Blue**

WEIGHT RANGE: **6–12 lb**

LIFE EXPECTANCY: **15 years**

CHARACTER: **Vocal, friendly, and smart**

Seal-points have dark brown markings—the color of a fur seal's pelt.

The pointing on the cat's face is called the mask. It grows bigger as the cat ages.

From East to West

The first Siamese cat arrived in the United States in 1878. It was a gift from the U.S. consul in Bangkok to the First Lady, Lucy Hayes. These early Siamese cats were seal-points. Today, the four accepted point colors are—from darkest to lightest—seal, chocolate, blue, and lilac.

The Exotic Shorthair is a cuddly lap cat. In the United States, only the Persian is more popular.

Like a Teddy Bear

The Siamese is lean and long—very different than the soft, rounded shape of other exotics. The Exotic Shorthair is like the Persian (see page 20) without the long coat. It is sometimes known as the "lazy person's Persian" because its coat does not tangle. The short, thick fur is as soft and plush as a teddy bear's!

EGYPTIAN MAU

The ancient Egyptians were among the first to keep tame, **domesticated** cats—there are even cats in ancient Egyptian temple and tomb paintings. Today's Egyptian Mau has been bred to resemble those first cats, which were relatives of the North African wildcat.

The Egyptian Mau is the only natural spotted breed of cat.

BREED PROFILE

NAME: **Egyptian Mau**

ORIGIN: **Egypt**

COLORS: **Silver, bronze, and smoke**

EYE COLORS: **Green**

WEIGHT RANGE: **6–11 lb**

LIFE EXPECTANCY: **15 years**

CHARACTER: **Shy, affectionate, and active**

Fast Cat

The Egyptian Mau still has some wild features, including cheetah-like speed. A long, loose flap of skin running from its ribcage to its back legs helps it to twist, jump, and accelerate. The Mau's hind legs are longer than its front ones, so it looks as if it is standing on tiptoe.

Striking Spots

The Mau is elegant and graceful, with a silky coat and striking pattern. It should have an "M" on its forehead and random but distinct spots. There is also a dark stripe that runs down the backbone to the tail.

The "M" is sometimes called the "mark of the scarab." Scarabs were beetles held sacred by the Egyptians.

IS THAT A CAT?

Cats are **mammals** and all mammals have hair or fur. However, natural **mutations** mean that some cats are born bald. Breeders have created some hairless breeds, including the Sphynx, the Donskoy, and the Peterbald. Other cats, such as the Cornish Rex, have very thin coats.

First Sphynx

In 1966, a black-and-white domestic cat gave birth to a hairless kitten in Toronto, Canada. Named Prune for its wrinkly skin, this was the first Sphynx cat. At first the breed was called the Canadian Hairless. Then it was renamed because of its resemblance to ancient Egyptian sculptures of sphinxes (beings that were half-human, half-cat).

BREED PROFILE

NAME: **Sphynx**

ORIGIN: **Canada**

COLORS: **All**

EYE COLORS: **All**

WEIGHT RANGE: **8–15 lb**

LIFE EXPECTANCY: **15 years**

CHARACTER: **Friendly, affectionate, and playful**

Some people love the Sphynx, but others find it too odd-looking!

16

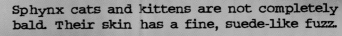

Sphynx cats and kittens are not completely bald. Their skin has a fine, suede-like fuzz.

Russian Rescue

The story of the Donskoy began when a Russian woman rescued a stray in the city of Rostov-on-Don. As the cat grew, she lost her hair. When she had kittens, some had hair and some didn't. Those that did lost it as they grew up.

The Donskoy's soft, wrinkled skin feels warm and velvety to the touch.

Rippled Rex

Most Cornish Rex kittens are born with rippled fur, but some lose it for a few weeks and look more like a Sphynx. The breed dates back to 1950 when a cat in Cornwall, England, gave birth to a kitten called Kallibunker. It had a slim body, long legs, and a very wavy coat.

This Cornish Rex has the typical short, wavy coat.

AMERICAN STARS

The names of these striking breeds proudly announce their origins. The American Wirehair and American Bobtail have both been around since the 1960s. The American Curl is a more recent breed, dating from the 1980s.

BREED PROFILE

NAME: **American Curl**

ORIGIN: **United States**

COLORS: **All**

EYE COLORS: **All**

WEIGHT RANGE: **7–11 lb**

LIFE EXPECTANCY: **15 years**

CHARACTER: **Sweet, gentle, and curious**

Curly-Eared Cat

A stray longhair with unusual ears was the founding mother of the American Curl breed. Today, there are long- and short-haired versions. In both, the ears curl back in an arc between 90 and 180 degrees.

This American Curl has a short, tabby spotted coat.

FELINE FACTS!

American Curls are born with straight ears. These are fully curled by the age of three months.

18

The long-haired American Curl has an elegant, plumed tail that looks like a feather boa!

Unique Coat

Its dense, crimped, and springy coat is what separates the American Wirehair from other cat breeds. This naturally occurring feature is seen from birth and seems to be unique to the United States.

If this American Wirehair mates with another American Wirehair, their kittens may have short or wiry hair.

Like a Wildcat

A kitten called Yodi started the American Bobtail breed. Named for its short, **bobbed** tail, the Bobtail is a muscular cat and the long-haired version looks particularly wild. However, the breed is friendly and affectionate and makes a good family pet.

An American Bobtail's tail can be as short as 1 inch, but no longer than its hock (the point on the hind leg).

FABULOUS AND FLUFFY

Long-haired cats are soft, silky, and wonderful to stroke. Some, such as the Persian, are centuries old. The Norwegian Forest Cat has distant origins, too. Its ancestor was kept by the Vikings as a pet and ship's cat.

The Norwegian Forest Cat's double-layered, waterproof coat can cope with Norway's harsh winters.

Prized Persians

As camel caravans of traders traveled through Persia (now Iran), their cargoes included striking cats with long, flowing fur. These longhairs look very different from the Norwegian Forest Cat because of their round, flat faces. The central position of their big, round eyes makes their faces resemble pansy flowers.

White Persians can have pale-blue or copper eyes—or be odd-eyed and have one of each!

The York Chocolate's semi-long coat is incredibly silky and soft. The fur is thicker at the ruff (chest and neck) and at the tops of the legs.

FELINE FACTS!

Vikings probably took cats with them when they briefly settled Vinland, North America, around 1000 CE.

Rich Chocolate

The York Chocolate has a rich, chocolate-brown or lavender coat, either solid or bicolored. Kittens are often paler in color. The breed has only been around since the 1980s and is named for New York State. It is shy but very affectionate and loves to be cuddled.

BREED PROFILE

NAME: **Norwegian Forest Cat**

ORIGIN: **Norway**

COLORS: **All**

EYE COLORS: **All**

WEIGHT RANGE: **12–16 lb**

LIFE EXPECTANCY: **14–16 years**

CHARACTER: **Playful, intelligent, and friendly**

MAINE COON

The Maine Coon was the first longhair to emerge naturally from the United States and it is the official state cat of Maine. The first recorded Maine Coon was a black-and-white cat that lived in the 1870s—it had the rather grand name of Captain Jenks of the Horse Marines!

Close Cousins?

Some believe that the Maine Coon's origins go back even further. When the Vikings sailed to America in the 11th century, they brought Norwegian Forest Cats with them. The two breeds look similar, so there may be some truth in this.

This illustration of a Maine Coon dates to the 1880s. It was used in an advertisement.

Thanks to its insulating coat, the Maine Coon can happily hunt in the snow!

Gentle Giant

The Maine Coon grows into the biggest cat breed in the world—adult males can measure 40 inches long. However, it truly is a gentle giant that loves people and other pets. It will happily play "Fetch" like a dog and can be walked on a leash. Unusually for a cat, it loves water and has water-resistant fur.

This huge Maine Coon is being shown off at a cat show in Kyrgyzstan.

FELINE FACTS!

Some people thought Maine Coons were the result of cats mating with raccoons!

Cat of Many Colors

Seventy-five colors are accepted in a registered Maine Coon, but the most common is brown tabby—a mixture of chocolate-brown, beige, cream, and every other shade of brown in between. Other colors include red, silver, tortoiseshell, smoke, and shaded.

The two tabby patterns are classic like this, with a mix of splotches, stripes, and swirls, or mackerel (striped).

23

SHORTHAIR BREEDS

When the Romans invaded the British Isles in 43 CE, they brought cats to keep down the rodents. Their cats bred with native wildcats to produce the British Shorthair. Today, it is the most popular breed in the United Kingdom.

The British Shorthair has a powerful body, a big, round head, and a short, thick coat.

American Shorthairs come in a huge range of colors. As adults, these silver tabby kittens will have green or hazel eyes.

Pilgrims' Pets

Domestic cats were not seen in North America from the time of the Viking settlement at Vinland until the Pilgrims arrived in the 1620s. Early settlers treasured cats as rat-catchers, but also as companions. By the late 19th century, the Domestic Shorthair was very valuable. In 1896, someone offered the enormous sum of $2,500 for a beautiful brown tabby at a cat show at Madison Square Garden in New York City!

Too Many Toes?

Cats born with more than the usual number of toes are described as **polydactyl**. The Pixiebob began about 30 years ago when a native wildcat, the red bobcat, mated with a polydactyl barn cat. The "Pixie" refers to the name of one of their kittens; the "bob" comes from the short, bobbed tail. Pixiebobs have a spotted tabby coat, from tawny to reddish brown.

Being polydactyl is very common in the Pixiebob—in fact, it is the breed standard.

FELINE FACTS!

Cats usually have 18 toes—five on each front paw and four on each hind—but an American cat called Jake had 28!

RARE BREEDS

Some breeds are incredibly rare. For example, there are fewer than 100 Kurilian Bobtails in North America. The Korat is hard to come by, too—would-be owners must join long waiting lists! The Sokoke is rarer still, with no more than 30 outside its native Kenya.

FELINE FACTS!

In Thailand, it is thought to be lucky to give a bride a pair of Korat cats on her wedding day.

Pacific Pets

Cats with short tails are known to have lived on the Kuril Islands in the North Pacific for at least 200 years. They were brought to mainland Russia in the 20th century but are still rarely seen outside Russian cat shows.

The Kuril Islands are volcanic islands that lie between the Japanese island of Hokkaido and the Russian Kamchatka Peninsula.

The Kurilian Bobtail can be long-haired like this one, or short-haired.

African Origins

The Sokoke comes from Kenya and looks a little like an ocelot, with typical blotchy tabby markings. It is one of the oldest, rarest breeds of domestic cat. In 2000, when the North American Sokoke Association was founded, there were only three individuals in the United States.

The Sokoke is named after the Kenyan forest where it originated.

BREED PROFILE

NAME: **Kurilian Bobtail**

ORIGIN: **Russia**

COLORS: **Tabby and self colors**

EYE COLORS: **All, including odd**

WEIGHT RANGE: **7–10 lb**

LIFE EXPECTANCY: **15 years**

CHARACTER: **Gentle, playful, and affectionate**

The Korat has a distinctive, heart-shaped head.

Silver Halo

The Korat's hair is dark blue-gray at the root, fading to silver at the tips, giving a shimmering, halo effect. The breed comes from Ampur Pimai in the Korat province of Thailand. Like the Siamese (see page 10), it was mentioned in the 14th-century *Cat Book Poems*.

FAR AND WIDE

Some pedigree cats are particularly prized for their good looks and refinement. The Abyssinian, Burmese, and Turkish Van come from as far away as Africa, Asia, and Europe, but they are all cat aristocracy!

Beginnings of the Burmese

Joseph Cheesman Thompson brought the first Burmese to the United States in 1930. It was a small, walnut-brown female named Wong Mau. Through careful breeding with seal-point Siamese cats, Thompson developed a cat with a unique, solid brown, or sable, coat. Later, other colors became acceptable.

The American Burmese has a short, rounded muzzle and a full face.

BREED PROFILE

BREED: Burmese

ORIGIN: Burma

COLORS: Sable, champagne, platinum, and blue

EYE COLORS: Copper and gold

WEIGHT RANGE: 8–14 lb

LIFE EXPECTANCY: 13 years

CHARACTER: Calm, playful, and kittenish

Swimming Cats

Turkish Van cats originate from near Lake Van in eastern Turkey and have a characteristic that sets them apart from most felines—they love to swim! Their soft coats feel like the finest cashmere but are completely waterproof.

The Turkish Van is white with a darker color on its head and tail.

AFFECTIONATE BREEDS

Cats are famous for being aloof and preferring their own company, but that is not true of all breeds. Ragdolls are one of the most affectionate. They seem to prefer people to cats and run to greet their owners at the door.

FELINE FACTS!

Ragdolls are named for the way they flop limply when picked up—like a child's cloth doll.

Ragdolls are always pointed. They can be bicolored, like this chocolate kitten, or have white mittens.

BREED PROFILE

NAME: **Ragdoll**

ORIGIN: **United States**

COLORS: **Six colors in four patterns**

EYE COLORS: **Blue, copper, and green**

WEIGHT RANGE: **15–20 lb**

LIFE EXPECTANCY: **12 years or more**

CHARACTER: **Affectionate, friendly, and quiet**

Scottish Rarity

Every bit as endearing as it looks, the Scottish Fold is a rare breed of cat with ears that fold flat to its head. The breed began when a shepherd named William Ross spotted a white cat with folded ears in Scotland, United Kingdom, and asked her owners if he could have one of her kittens. Scottish Fold kittens are born with straight ears; the ears fold by the age of three weeks.

The Scottish Fold has widely spaced eyes.

Unlike the Siamese, the Himalayan does not demand attention—but it does love to be cuddled!

Lovable Longhair

The Himalayan has the long hair, stocky body, and snub-nosed face of a Persian, with the striking points and dark-blue eyes of a Siamese. This enchanting, lovable cat has a thick **double coat** that becomes matted without regular brushing.

BEAUTIFUL BLUES

From dark smokes to glimmering grays, blue coats in cats are highly prized. The Russian Blue has plush fur that comes in various shades of blue, always with a silvery sheen. It was rumored to be the cat of choice for Russian royalty.

The Russian Blue was first seen in the United States in the early 20th century.

In the earliest English cat shows, Russian Blues competed against blue British Shorthairs like this one.

An American Hit

Russian Blues were taken to the United States in the early 1900s, but were not bred in any numbers until after the Second World War (1939–45). The breed soon became as popular for its sweet nature as for its exotic good looks.

FELINE FACTS!

The Russian Blue is also called the Archangel Cat, because it was first seen by non-Russians at Arkhangelsk, a Russian seaport.

Germanic Longhair

The Nebelung is a long-haired version of the Russian Blue, with a shimmering, silver-tipped blue coat and vivid, yellow-green eyes. The first pair were bred from a black domestic shorthair and a black longhair, possibly a Turkish Angora. They were named Siegfried and Brunhilde after characters in *Song of the Nibelungs*, an old German poem.

The German word *Nebel* means "haze" or "mist."

CUTE AND CURLY

The Rex breeds are often called "cats in sheep's clothing" because of their curly coats. The newest is the Selkirk Rex, which started with a curly-coated kitten named Miss DePesto (Pest for short!) in Montana in 1987.

This is the long-haired version of the Selkirk Rex.

Waves and Curls

The Selkirk Rex is named after Montana's Selkirk Mountains. Its thick, soft coat is usually curliest around the neck and belly. The Selkirk does not have uniform rows of tight curls like some Rex breeds.

It can take up to two years for the Selkirk Rex's curly coat to fully develop.

FELINE FACTS!

All American Curl cats trace back to one stray kitten called Shulamith.

34

Bald Beginnings

The LaPerm breed also dates to the 1980s—the founding mother was born to a barn cat in the Columbia River Gorge. The kitten did not look promising; she was long and skinny, with huge ears, and she was bald, with tabby markings on her skin. However, within eight weeks she had grown soft, wavy hair. Called Curly, she went on to have litters of bald kittens that formed the LaPerm breed.

The LaPerm's long, shaggy coat comes in all colors, shades, and patterns.

BREED PROFILE

NAME: Selkirk Rex

ORIGIN: North America

COLORS: All

EYE COLORS: All

WEIGHT RANGE: 7–11 lb

LIFE EXPECTANCY: 14 years

CHARACTER: Sweet, gentle, and playful

All in the Ears

The American Curl does not boast a curly coat; instead, it is named for its pretty, curled ears that give it a charmingly surprised expression. This breed is nicknamed the Peter Pan of the cat world because it stays kittenish into adulthood.

The long-haired American Curl has a soft, silky coat.

CATS IN MINIATURE

Big is not always beautiful—some cats are bred to be small. Munchkins, known for their short, stubby legs, developed in the 1980s. Since then, they have been crossbred to create other short-legged breeds, such as the Lambkin Dwarf (half-Selkirk Rex), Skookum (half-LaPerm), and Bambino (half-Sphynx).

Feline Pixie

With its large ears, big eyes, short muzzle, and high cheekbones, the Devon Rex has been nicknamed the "pixie cat." It comes from Devon, in southwest England, where a feral tomcat with a curly coat mated with a pet cat, and one of the kittens had the same curls. Despite similarities, it is not related to the Cornish Rex, from the neighboring county in England.

The Devon Rex is a small cat but it has huge, pixie-like ears.

Impish Angel

The little Singapura originates from Singapore in Southeast Asia and has a distinctive, ticked brown coat. It can weigh as little as 4 pounds, but its legs are relatively long. It has an angelic face, sparkling eyes, and a very mischievous personality!

BREED PROFILE

NAME: **Munchkin**

ORIGIN: **United States**

COLORS: **All**

EYE COLORS: **All**

WEIGHT RANGE: **6–9 lb**

LIFE EXPECTANCY: **15 years**

CHARACTER: **Playful, loving, and curious**

The Singapura comes only in sepia agouti—seal-brown ticking on ivory.

On such short legs, the Munchkin cannot leap long distances, but it is an energetic climber.

FELINE FACTS!

Munchkin cats are named after the small, childlike people that appear in *The Wonderful Wizard of Oz*.

OLD BLUE EYES

Several cat breeds are known for their blue eyes—the gene is most common in solid white cats and ones with pointed markings. White cats with blue eyes are often deaf.

Sacred Cat

A legend connects the Birman to a temple in Burma, where white long-haired cats were considered sacred. According to the story, the high priest's cat had chased off some thieves with a hiss. Later, as the priest died, his soul entered the body of the brave cat and the cat's eyes turned a dazzling blue.

This fluffy little Birman is still only a kitten.

FELINE FACTS!

One of the rarest blue-eyed breeds is the Ojos Azules from New Mexico, USA. Its name means "blue eyes" in Spanish.

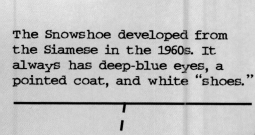

The Snowshoe developed from the Siamese in the 1960s. It always has deep-blue eyes, a pointed coat, and white "shoes."

A Dancer's Grace

The Balinese is a long-haired version of the Siamese. Its origins are Thailand, not the Indonesian island of Bali—the name comes from the cat's gracefulness, which reminded the first breeder of elegant Balinese dancers. Its long, silky coat seems to flow over its slender body.

The Balinese is a very energetic cat. It can become destructive if left on its own for long periods of time.

BREED PROFILE

NAME: **Snowshoe**

ORIGIN: **United States**

COLORS: **All pointed colors**

EYE COLORS: **Blue**

WEIGHT RANGE: **6–12 lb**

LIFE EXPECTANCY: **12–15 years**

CHARACTER: **Sociable, lively, and affectionate**

39

ON THE WILD SIDE

All modern breeds are related to wildcats—but some are closer relatives than others! The slinky Savannah, for example, began with a kitten born to a pet Siamese but fathered by a serval, a wildcat of the savanna (Africa's grassy plains).

FELINE FACTS!

The word "chausie" means "jungle cat."

A male Chausie can grow to 22 pounds. This one is a brown, spotted tabby.

Choice Chausie

The jungle cat is another small wildcat. It is found across southern Asia, the Middle East, and in northeast Africa. By crossing a jungle cat with a pet cat, the Chausie was created. It became a recognized breed in 1995. It is large, muscular, and very active.

The Savannah has a long neck and legs, large ears and bold markings.

The Toyger's coat comes with mackerel stripes.

Tiger Stripes

With its vivid stripes and rolling gait, the Toyger resembles a wild tiger in miniature. Despite its name, it doesn't have a single drop of real tiger blood in its heritage! It is a fairly new breed, and is still being developed so that it has those beautiful, well-defined stripes. But it is a friendly, happy cat that loves being with people.

THE BENGAL

The exotic-looking Bengal is the only domestic cat that has the rosette markings of wildcats. Originally named the Leopardette, it is the result of matings between pet cats and the Asian leopard cat.

BREED PROFILE

NAME: **Bengal**

ORIGIN: **United States**

COLORS: **All shades of brown, ivory, or white, with leopard spots or marbling**

EYE COLORS: **Blue, green, and gold**

WEIGHT RANGE: **12–22 lb**

LIFE EXPECTANCY: **16 years**

CHARACTER: **Friendly, alert, and intelligent**

Part of the Family

The Bengal loves to play—it will jump and turn somersaults, bounce around, and climb doors and curtains. It likes to feel like part of the family, so it will insist on joining in with whatever its owner is doing, including answering the door or taking a bath! It is quite **vocal**—if you ask one a question, it will usually coo, chirp, or yowl in reply!

The Bengal has dark "eyeliner" markings around the eyes.

This playful Bengal kitten is only a few months old.

Wild Cousin

Scientists created the Bengal by accident. They were hoping to breed pet cats that would not catch **feline leukemia**. Asia's most widespread wildcat, the Asian leopard cat, is naturally immune to the disease.

The Asian leopard cat has adapted to different habitats, including forests, mountains, scrub, and semidesert.

43

MARVELOUS MIXES

Crossbreeding isn't always deliberate—sometimes a new cross is a complete accident. The beautiful Burmilla began after a lilac Burmese escaped and mated with a Persian Chinchilla. The four black-and-silver kittens were so pretty that a breeding program started.

This RagaMuffin has tabby markings. The breed can also be tortoiseshell or bicolored.

Calm Beauty

The RagaMuffin is much like the Ragdoll, but it is accepted as a pure breed in its own right. Like the Ragdoll, it weighs up to 20 pounds. It has large, expressive eyes and a wonderfully thick, soft coat. Its sweet, calm nature makes it a perfect pet for families with children.

Kittenish Character

Created in the United States, the Tonkinese was first known as the "chocolate Siamese." It is actually a cross between a Siamese and Burmese. The breed is affectionate and playful. It behaves like a kitten throughout its life and is also good with other pets—even dogs!

The oriental-looking Tonkinese has a slim body, an angular face, and almond eyes.

FELINE FACTS!
The Tonkinese was the first pedigree cat to have aqua-colored eyes.

The Burmese kitten has a background color of silver or gold with shaded fur—in this case, in lilac.

45

FROM KITTEN TO CAT

Mother cats usually give birth to about four kittens—although a litter can contain just one or more than a dozen! For the first couple of days, the mother hardly leaves her helpless babies. Then they grow stronger and start to become more adventurous.

The newborns find their mother's teats by smell.

Mother's Milk

Kittens are blind and deaf when they are born. Their eyes and ears won't open for a few weeks. The kittens feed on their mother's milk, just like all baby mammals. At six or seven weeks they are **weaned**, or moved off milk and onto solid food.

Play-fighting helps kittens to develop the skills they will need as hunters.

Serious Play

Kittens are little bundles of energy. First they toddle and tumble. By four weeks, they can walk, and by five, they can run. Play teaches vital hunting skills. The kittens stalk, pounce, chase their own tails, and ambush each other. They learn their **pecking order** in the litter.

Littermates can be different colors as they inherit genes from both parents.

Into Adulthood

Kittens grow quickly. Most are adults by the age of one—able to reproduce and have kittens of their own. Loved and looked after properly, cats can live for 20 years or more.

As cats age, they usually become less active.

47

CAT CARE

Every cat is different, but each has the same basic needs: food, warmth, shelter, social interaction, and love. Although cats have been pets for thousands of years, they still have some wild habits, too.

Feeding Your Cat

Unlike dogs, cats must have meat to survive. Pet cats are usually fed twice a day. Many have a diet of wet food, sometimes with dry biscuits sprinkled on top for crunch. Cats with weak gums eat only dried food in order to keep their mouths healthy.

Cats need access to a bowl of drinking water, too.

FELINE FACTS!
Cats have 30 teeth (compared to a dog's 42) and they are almost all adapted to eat meat.

48

Scratching stops the cat's claws from growing too long. It also leaves behind signals for other cats to see and smell.

Cat Health

Even healthy cats must visit the veterinarian once a year for a check-up and **booster vaccinations**. He or she also treats cats that are unwell or injured. The veterinarian can **neuter** male or female cats to prevent unwanted kittens.

A head cone like this stops the cat from licking a wound while it heals.

Cat Talk

Cats have different ways to communicate. They let their owner know what they want with a range of noises, including meows, chirps, purrs, trills, hisses, yowls, and growls. When cats scratch or rub their cheeks on things, they are leaving a mark on their **territory** to show other cats that it is theirs. Males will **spray** for the same reason, unless they are neutered.

Cats make a range of noises, but cannot produce the roar of their big cat cousins.

49

ALL ABOUT DOGS

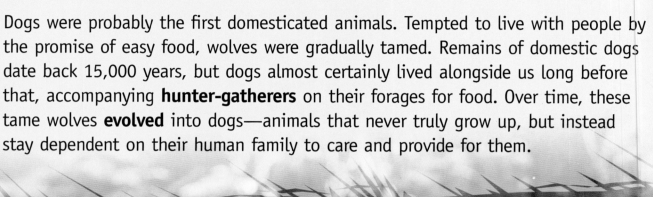

Dogs were probably the first domesticated animals. Tempted to live with people by the promise of easy food, wolves were gradually tamed. Remains of domestic dogs date back 15,000 years, but dogs almost certainly lived alongside us long before that, accompanying **hunter-gatherers** on their forages for food. Over time, these tame wolves **evolved** into dogs—animals that never truly grow up, but instead stay dependent on their human family to care and provide for them.

DOG DATA!

Modern dogs are so similar to gray wolves that the two species can breed with each other.

Along with all other
modern dog breeds,
these German Shepherds
belong to the same
family as wolves,
jackals, and coyotes.

DOGS IN THE WILD

The gray wolf lives across North America—in Canada, Alaska, the Great Lakes, the northern Rockies, and the Pacific Northwest—as well as in parts of Europe, Asia, and Africa. It is the domestic dog's ancestor, but it is just one member of the dog family.

Wily Coyote

The coyote or prairie wolf is smaller than its cousin the gray wolf. Found across North America, Mexico, and Central America, this smart animal has adapted to many different habitats. A coyote will hunt alone as well as in family groups. It has superb sight, a strong sense of smell, and will eat almost anything!

The gray wolf usually lives in packs of about seven animals. However, the largest wolf packs have been known to have more than 40!

The coyote feeds on mice, rabbits, lizards, insects, and fruit.

Endangered Pack Animal

Once found across Africa, the African hunting dog is now an endangered species. It lives in family groups of up to 40 animals, although most contain only about a dozen dogs. It hunts together in packs and can reach sprinting speeds of up to 44 miles per hour.

African hunting dogs are also known as painted wolves because their coats seem to have different colors splashed on.

DOG DATA!

African hunting dogs have only four toes on their front feet; all other members of the dog family have five.

The dingo is Australia's largest land predator.

Dog Down Under

Australia's wild dog, the dingo, probably reached the continent with seafarers from Asia around 4,000 years ago. It preys on rabbits, rats, and kangaroos, but it also steals farmers' livestock.

53

FABULOUS FOXES

Foxes are the world's most common wild dog. The most northerly species is the Arctic fox. Its short ears, short muzzle, and furry-soled feet protect it from the cold and its white winter coat provides camouflage against the snow.

In the summer months, the Arctic becomes tundra, and the fox's fur turns brown or gray.

Red foxes are amazingly agile. They also have sharp hearing and night vision.

Town and Country

The red fox is the biggest species of fox. Despite its name, it comes in a variety of colors, including silvery gray. It is found across the northern half of the world. As well as the countryside, the red fox lives in towns and cities, where it hunts rodents and raids garbage cans for food.

Enormous Ears

The smallest fox species, the fennec fox, lives in the hot Sahara Desert, North Africa. Its six-inch-long ears help it to lose body heat and keep cool. The fennec fox also has an excellent sense of hearing, able to pick up the sounds of insects or small mammals moving around under the sand.

The tiny fennec fox weighs just a few pounds.

DOG COLORS

Some dog breeds only come in certain colors—others may be all sorts of colors and patterns.

Colors commonly seen include:

Self or Solid

Each hair on the dog is the same color all the way along.

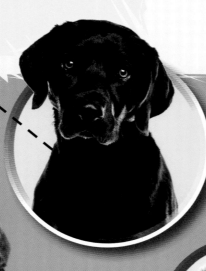

black

silver gray

fawn

apricot

widow's peak

cross on chest

Markings

White or black hairs form a pattern, such as a chest cross or a "V" shape on the head (a widow's peak).

odd

blue

Eye Colors

Most dogs have brown or dark brown eyes. A few breeds, such as the Collie or Husky, may have blue. Huskies have odd-colored eyes, too.

Patterns

Freckles, patches, and spots are just some of the amazing coat patterns.

salt-and-pepper

blue roan

liver belton

spotted

brindle

Color Combinations

Coats can be bicolored (two colors), particolored (one main color with patches in one or more other colors), or tricolored (three colors).

bicolored
(black and white)

bicolored
(black and tan)

particolored
(white
with tan
patches)

Blenheim (white
with chestnut
patches)

tricolored
(black, white,
and tan)

ANCIENT BREEDS

Since prehistoric times, people have kept dogs to guard their possessions and livestock and to help them hunt. The Basenji is a hunting dog from Africa. The pharaohs of ancient Egypt kept Basenji. The oldest sculpture of one dates back to 4000 BCE.

Livestock Protector

The Kuvasz is the oldest of Hungary's dog breeds. Large and protective, it was popular with shepherds because its stunning white coat made it easy to tell apart from the wolves that stalked sheep.

The Kuvasz can trot nonstop for more than 15 miles without tiring.

58

BREED PROFILE

NAME: Basenji

ORIGIN: North Africa

COLORS: Red and white, black and white, tricolored, and brindle

EYE COLORS: Hazel to dark brown

WEIGHT RANGE: 22–24 lb

LIFE EXPECTANCY: 12 years

CHARACTER: Playful, alert, and loving

A Riot of Wrinkles

Dogs resembling the Shar Pei appear on Chinese pots dating back more than 2,000 years. The first thing you notice about this breed is its wrinkles—it appears to be wearing a coat several sizes too big! The Chinese used it as a guard and fighting dog. In a fight, its opponent could not make a flesh wound as it simply got a mouthful of flabby skin.

The Shar Pei's coat is short, bristly, and rough. It feels like sandpaper to the touch.

The Basenji is a sleek dog with a tightly curled tail. It keeps itself clean like a cat.

AFGHAN

As its name suggests, the Afghan comes from Afghanistan in the Middle East. It is an old breed, dating back at least 4,000 years. It is a kind of hound—its agility and speed meant it was used to hunt deer, gazelle, goats, and wild boar. It also protected its masters from wolves and snow leopards.

The Afghan is a sighthound (see page 76), which means it hunts by sight.

Regal and Swift

The Afghan's luxuriant fur makes it instantly recognizable. Other breed traits are its narrow, regal face with its dark mask, and the high hipbones that help it achieve great speed. It is closely related to the Greyhound, and Afghan owners like to race their dogs.

Over short distances, the Afghan can reach speeds of 43 miles per hour.

DOG DATA!

The Afghan was the first dog to be cloned. The clone, called "Snuppy," was born in South Korea in 2005.

BREED PROFILE

NAME: **Afghan**

ORIGIN: **Afghanistan**

COLORS: **Gold, brown, black, cream, blue, brindle, and white**

EYE COLORS: **Dark brown or hazel**

WEIGHT RANGE: **50–60 lb**

LIFE EXPECTANCY: **14 years**

CHARACTER: **Alert, lively, and reserved**

Glamorous Coat

The Afghan's long, glossy coat is its finest feature, but takes a lot of looking after. The dog benefits from regular bathing, but too much brushing can damage the fur, making it more prone to matting. The long hair kept the Afghan warm in its native home, the harsh mountains of Afghanistan.

The Afghan's whole body is covered in long, silky hair—even its feet.

61

RARE BREEDS

Some dog breeds are common everywhere. Others are known only in one part of the world. Brazil's national dog, the Fila Brasileiro, is a fierce guard dog that has been bred for hundreds of years. However, in many places, including the United States, it is not recognized as a pedigree breed.

DOG DATA!
In Brazil there is a saying, "as faithful as a Fila." The dog is known for its amazing loyalty.

Dog for Ducks

The Kooikerhondje is a **gundog** from the Netherlands, traditionally used to tempt ducks out of the water for hunters. It is thought to be an ancestor of the Nova Scotia Duck Toller (see page 67). Dogs very like the Kooikerhondje appear in Dutch paintings from the 17th century. The breed nearly died out in the 20th century and is still rare.

The black tips on the Kooikerhondje's long ears are known as "earrings."

Desert Hound

Azawakhs are kept by the nomadic Tuareg and Fula tribes of the Sahara Desert and West Africa. The dogs guard their cattle against hyenas and other predators. They also hunt gazelles and wild hares for the people to eat. The Azawakh makes a loyal pet, but is very rare, partly because it suffers in colder climates.

The Azawakh has a long neck, a narrow, hound-like head, and pendant (hanging) ears.

BREED PROFILE

BREED: **Azawakh**

ORIGIN: **North Africa**

COLORS: **Fawn, sand, brindle, blue, white, and brown**

EYE COLORS: **Dark brown**

WEIGHT RANGE: **33–55 lb**

LIFE EXPECTANCY: **15 years**

CHARACTER: **Active, loyal, and strong-willed**

Also known as the Brazilian Mastiff, the Fila Brasileiro is outstanding at tracking, herding, and guarding.

63

IS THAT A DOG?

The Chinese Crested has a very playful personality.

Hairlessness in dogs was a natural mutation. Several breeds have been deliberately developed to be bald. A dog that cannot shed hair is a good choice for people with allergies. There are other advantages, too—bald dogs have less odor than hairy ones and they cannot harbor fleas.

BREED PROFILE

NAME: **Chinese Crested**

ORIGIN: **China**

COLORS: **Black, chocolate, blue, tricolored, cream, and apricot**

EYE COLORS: **Brown, green, blue, black, and odd**

WEIGHT RANGE: **Up to 11 lb**

LIFE EXPECTANCY: **15 years**

CHARACTER: **Happy, loving, and alert**

Hairless and Powderpuff

The Chinese Crested Dog comes in two varieties. The Hairless has a crest of hair on its head and neck, "socks" that cover its toes, and a plume on its tail. The rest of its body has no hair at all and its skin needs to be moisturized regularly. The Powderpuff is evenly covered with long, fine hair. Both types can be born in the same litter.

The Powderpuff Chinese Crested has a long, soft coat and needs daily grooming.

Mesoamerican Idol

Also known as the Mexican Hairless, the Xoloitzcuintli (pronounced "shoh-loyts-kweent-lee") is one of the oldest dog breeds. It was kept by the Maya and the Aztecs. It was saved from extinction in the 1950s and today comes in three different sizes: miniature (10–14 inches at the shoulder), intermediate (14–18 inches), and standard (18–24 inches). Not all Xoloitzcuintlis are hairless; some are born with a very fine, flat coat.

The Mexican Hairless has straggly tufts of hair on its forehead.

DOG DATA!

The Maya and Aztecs held the Xoloitzcuintli to be sacred. They thought it had healing powers.

LOYAL RETRIEVERS

DOG DATA!

The Chesapeake Bay Retriever breed began with two puppies that were rescued from a shipwreck.

Retrievers are a kind of gundog. Hunters use them to retrieve game animals that they have shot. The Golden Retriever was developed by a Scottish baron in the mid- to late-19th century to bring back shot pheasants and other game birds.

Popular Pet

Today, the Golden Retriever is one of the most popular dog breeds in the world. Still used as a working retriever, it is also used as a **sniffer dog** and **assistance dog** because it is so intelligent and easy to train.

The Golden Retriever's coat ranges from cream to deep yellow.

BREED PROFILE

NAME: **Golden Retriever**

ORIGIN: **Scotland, UK**

COLORS: **Light cream to golden**

EYE COLORS: **Dark brown and deep amber**

WEIGHT RANGE: **55–75 lb**

LIFE EXPECTANCY: **12 years**

CHARACTER: **Brave, trainable, and friendly**

Both intelligent and loving, the Golden Retriever is a popular choice as a pet.

Wavy-Coated and Waterproof

The Chesapeake Bay Retriever is the standard of all waterproof dogs. It is happiest in water—the colder the better! Its dense, oily coat repels water just like the feathers of a duck. It even has webbing between its toes to help it swim. Chesapeakes are very trainable and obedient, but they do need a lot of exercise.

The Chesapeake's curly coat can be brown, red-gold, or straw-colored.

Decoy Dog

The Nova Scotia Duck Tolling Retriever, or Toller, has a clever trick. Tolling means luring ducks or geese toward nets or guns, and the dog does this by waving its plumy, white-tipped tail. Like the Chesapeake, the Toller also has a thick, waterproof coat and webbed feet.

One of the Toller's favorite games is retrieving a ball from the water.

LABRADOR RETRIEVER

The popular Labrador Retriever is descended from the black dogs bred by fishermen off Newfoundland in Canada during the 18th and 19th centuries. The dogs fetched ropes, helped to haul in nets, and retrieved any fish that had wriggled off hooks.

Origins

A few of these fishermen's dogs were taken to England in the 19th century and these founded the modern breed. There is only one kind of Labrador, but breeders describe heavier, bigger Labradors as "English-type" and more athletic, working dogs as "American-type."

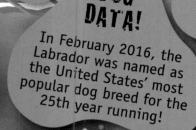

The Labrador's short, thick coat is designed to repel water.

The English-type Labrador Retriever has a slightly thicker neck and broader chest.

Powerful Physique

The Labrador has a unique tail shaped like an otter's (thick at the base and narrow at the tip) that helps to power it through the water when it is swimming. Its body is strong and sturdy and it has a waterproof double coat.

Muscular legs allow the Labrador to sprint, leap, and swim.

BREED PROFILE

NAME: **Labrador Retriever**

ORIGIN: **Canada**

COLORS: **Yellow, black, and chocolate**

EYE COLORS: **Dark brown, green, and yellow**

WEIGHT RANGE: **55–82 lb**

LIFE EXPECTANCY: **12 years**

CHARACTER: **Loyal, loving, and energetic**

The silver Labrador is a paler form of the chocolate one.

Controversial Colors

As well as the original black, Labradors come in chocolate or yellow. Their coats may also be white, fox-red (a darker version of the yellow), or silver, but none of these are officially recognized as pedigree colors.

WELSH CORGIS

Corgis are the smallest of the herding dog breeds. Despite the short legs, they are extremely agile, which made them good at herding cattle, sheep, and ponies. The breed began in Wales and today there are two kinds: the Pembroke and the Cardigan Corgi.

The Pembroke Welsh Corgi is the most popular as a pet.

Made in Wales

The Welsh Corgi was only split into two separate breeds in the 1930s. The Cardigan Corgi is the oldest of the two, dating back to the 1100s. It has larger ears and a longer body than the Pembroke. Both breeds stand no more than 12 inches high.

Red is the most common coat color for the Pembroke Welsh Corgi. All colors have a white "trim."

Yard-Long Dog

In Welsh, *cor* means "dwarf" and *gi* means "dog." The Corgi was also known as the "yard dog," not because it lived outside in the yard, but because the old breed (the Cardigan Corgi) measured one Welsh yard from its nose to the tip of its tail.

The Cardigan Welsh Corgi has very large, upright ears.

Regal Pet

Queen Elizabeth II of the United Kingdom is known for her love of Corgis. She has owned more than 30 during her lifetime. She also keeps Dorgis—crosses between Dachshunds and Corgis. The Dorgi can inherit characteristics from either of the parent breeds.

A footman takes a Dorgi (right) and Corgi (left) for a walk in the palace gardens.

71

SILKY SETTERS

The Setters are gundogs specially bred for hunting grouse, quail, pheasants, and other game birds. They are named for their habit of crouching very still ("setting") near birds. This shows their location so that the hunters know where to shoot.

The Irish Setter used to be known as the Red Setter because of its distinctive, flame-red coat.

Oldest Setter

Setter dogs have been around for centuries but were not separated into different breeds until the 1900s. The dogs that formed the modern English Setter were bred by a man called Edward Laverack in the 1820s. They are white with dark, dappled flecks in a range of colors including blue, black, orange, and tan.

This English Setter's coat— white with black flecks—is called "blue belton."

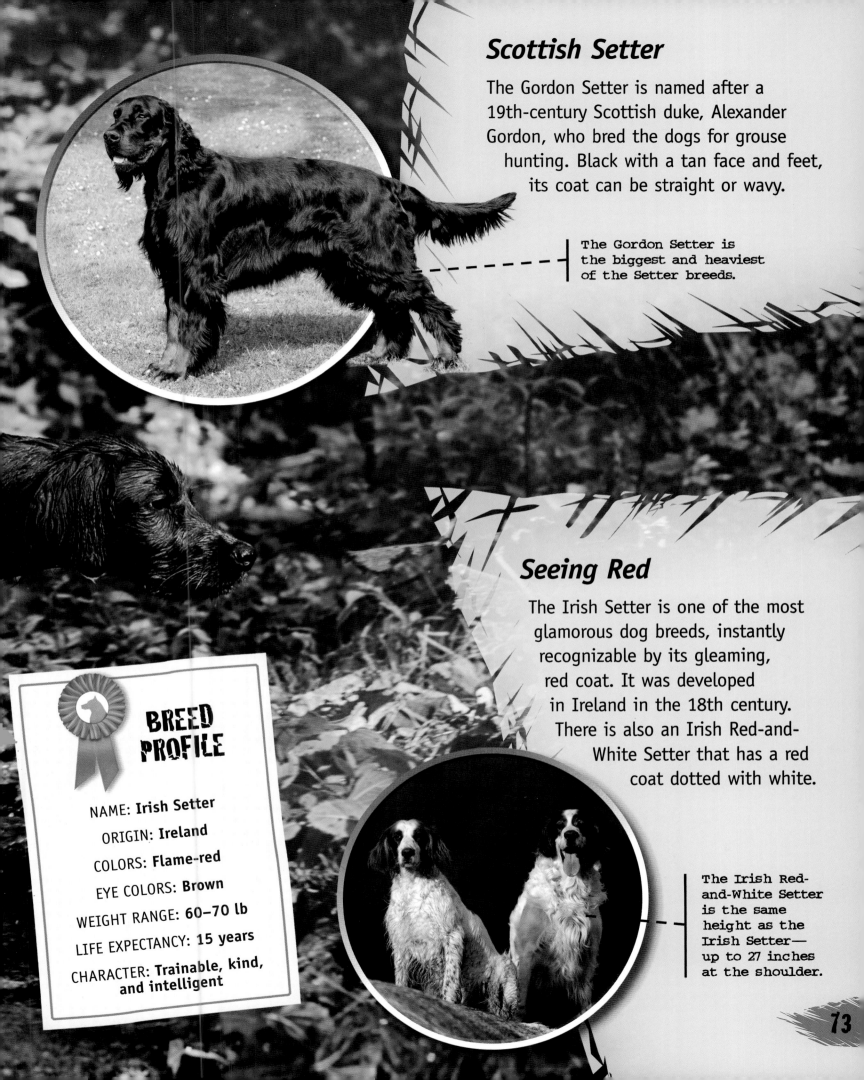

Scottish Setter

The Gordon Setter is named after a 19th-century Scottish duke, Alexander Gordon, who bred the dogs for grouse hunting. Black with a tan face and feet, its coat can be straight or wavy.

The Gordon Setter is the biggest and heaviest of the Setter breeds.

Seeing Red

The Irish Setter is one of the most glamorous dog breeds, instantly recognizable by its gleaming, red coat. It was developed in Ireland in the 18th century. There is also an Irish Red-and-White Setter that has a red coat dotted with white.

The Irish Red-and-White Setter is the same height as the Irish Setter—up to 27 inches at the shoulder.

BREED PROFILE

NAME: **Irish Setter**

ORIGIN: **Ireland**

COLORS: **Flame-red**

EYE COLORS: **Brown**

WEIGHT RANGE: **60–70 lb**

LIFE EXPECTANCY: **15 years**

CHARACTER: **Trainable, kind, and intelligent**

DINKY DACHSHUNDS

Intelligent and loyal, the Dachshund was bred in Germany more than 400 years ago to go into holes after foxes and badgers, and to track injured animals such as deer. Its name means "badger dog" in German.

Sizes and Coats

The Dachshund comes in three sizes, based on how big a hole it could fit into. Dachshunds can have three different coats, too. They can be long-haired, smooth-haired, or wire-haired.

This long-haired Dachshund has a red coat with black shading.

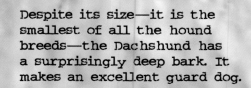

Despite its size—it is the smallest of all the hound breeds—the Dachshund has a surprisingly deep bark. It makes an excellent guard dog.

Plucky Pup

The Miniature Dachshund is a happy, active little dog. It is also fearless, and will attack animals much bigger than itself—a trait that was bred into it for hunting badgers, which can be ferocious. It will take as much exercise as you can give it, but will be just as happy curled up asleep on your lap.

BREED PROFILE

NAME: **Standard Dachshund**

ORIGIN: **Germany**

COLORS: **Black and tan, red, and silver dapple**

EYE COLORS: **Brown**

WEIGHT RANGE: **20–26 lb**

LIFE EXPECTANCY: **12 years**

CHARACTER: **Loyal, brave, and active**

This exuberant black-and-tan wire-haired Dachshund is on the trail

Sniffing Power

As a member of the hound family, the Dachshund has an excellent sense of smell. It can follow an injured deer or wild boar for up to two days after sniffing just a few drops of the animal's blood.

75

ELEGANT HOUNDS

Hounds are hunting dogs that help people to track or chase prey. Sighthounds are sleek, speedy breeds that keep prey in sight as they give chase. They include the Saluki and Borzoi.

Sleek Saluki

The Saluki comes from the Middle East. Bedouin nomads carried Salukis on their camels, and used them to hunt desert hare or gazelle. Traditionally, Salukis were never sold for money. They could only be given or swapped.

The Saluki sat in a purpose-built bag on the camel's saddle.

DOG DATA!

The Saluki was named for either the now-lost Arabian city of Saluk, or the town of Seleukia in ancient Syria.

Russian Greyhound

Saint Sophia's Cathedral in Kiev, Ukraine, houses 11th-century paintings that show long-haired hounds like the Borzoi chasing wild boar and stag. In the 19th century, Russian rulers and nobles used packs of up to 100 Borzoi to hunt wolves on the snowy tundra.

Lighter-colored Borzoi were most prized because they did not stand out against the snow.

This Saluki race is taking place at a camel festival near Abu Dhabi, United Arab Emirates.

Maltese Rabbiter

Another ancient breed, the Pharaoh Hound comes from Malta, an island in the Mediterranean Sea, where it was used to hunt rabbits. With its pricked-up ears, it resembles the jackal-headed ancient Egyptian god Anubis. Phoenician traders probably brought the first hounds to Malta around 1000 BCE.

The Pharaoh Hound may have a white chest and **stop**. The rest of its coat is tan to chestnut.

FAST BREEDS

Many hunting dogs are built for speed—not only sighthounds, such as the Saluki and Greyhound, but also sleek and powerful gundogs, such as the Vizsla and the Weimaraner. All of these dogs need plenty of exercise every day.

BREED PROFILE

NAME: **Hungarian Vizsla**

ORIGIN: **Hungary**

COLORS: **Red-gold**

EYE COLORS: **Dark brown**

WEIGHT RANGE: **44–66 lb**

LIFE EXPECTANCY: **15 years**

CHARACTER: **Energetic, loving, and eager to please**

Stuck on You

The Vizsla was bred by the Magyar people who settled in Hungary at the end of the 9th century. They used it to find and retrieve game. Sleek and muscular, the Vizsla has plenty of energy to burn off. It is nicknamed the "Velcro dog" because it sticks so closely to its owner.

The Vizsla also comes in a shaggy, wire-haired version.

Also known as the Hungarian Pointer, the Vizsla is intelligent and affectionate.

Silver Ghost

The Weimaraner's physique is very similar to the Vizsla's—the difference is its color. While the Vizsla is always a rusty-red, the Weimaraner's coat is an unusual silver-gray. The Weimaraner takes its name from the German court of Weimar, where it was highly prized.

Bouncy and boisterous, the Weimaraner is most popular as a shorthair, but can also be long-haired.

Sporty Racer

Despite its name, the Greyhound comes in a wide variety of colors, not only gray. It was originally bred as a hunting dog. In the 20th century, greyhound racing became a popular spectator sport in many parts of the world.

Racing greyhounds usually retire by the age of six. They they can live to be up to 12 years old.

MIGHTY MASTIFFS

Mastiffs belong to the molosser group of dog breeds, which are all large and solidly built. They take their name from the Molossus, a now-extinct war dog used by the ancient Greeks and Romans. It was probably introduced to England by the Romans.

BREED PROFILE

NAME: **Neapolitan Mastiff**

ORIGIN: **Italy**

COLORS: **Gray, blue, black, brown, tawny, and brindle**

EYE COLORS: **Dark brown**

WEIGHT RANGE: **110–154 lb**

LIFE EXPECTANCY: **10 years**

CHARACTER: **Affectionate, brave, and gentle**

Italian Heavyweight

With its massive size, multiple wrinkles, and imposing stare, the Neapolitan Mastiff looks scary. It is one of the world's heaviest dogs, weighing as much as a man. It traces its ancestry to the Tibetan Mastiff (see pages 82–83), but comes from Naples in southern Italy.

Gray and blue are the most popular coat colors for the Neapolitan Mastiff.

The English Mastiff has a huge, heavy head. Like most mastiffs, it is prone to drooling and slobbering.

Mountain Guard

The Phoenicians brought the Pyrenean Mastiff to the Pyrenees of northern Spain about 3,000 years ago. Its job was to protect flocks of sheep from wolves and bears as they were moved between their winter and summer pastures.

The Pyrenean Mastiff's thick fur provided protection in its cold mountain home.

DOG DATA!

The heaviest-ever dog was an English Mastiff called Zorba, who weighed 343 pounds.

TIBETAN MASTIFF

The mighty Tibetan Mastiff comes from the mountain valleys of the Himalayas. It was kept by nomadic sheep herders and traders and it guarded their tents from wolves, snow leopards, and other predators.

Arrival in England

The region of Tibet lies in the far west of China, bordering India and Nepal. It is extremely isolated. Little was known about its dogs until 1847, when Lord Hardinge, Viceroy of India, sent a "large dog from Tibet" to Queen Victoria of Great Britain. Her son (later King Edward VII) brought two more Tibetan Mastiffs into England in 1874.

This Tibetan Mastiff guards a mountain temple in Sichuan, southwestern China.

BREED PROFILE

NAME: **Tibetan Mastiff**

ORIGIN: **Tibet, China**

COLORS: **Black-and-tan, black, brown, blue-gray, gold, and red**

EYE COLORS: **Brown**

WEIGHT RANGE: **180–220 lb**

LIFE EXPECTANCY: **12 years**

CHARACTER: **Intelligent, protective, and gentle**

The Tibetan Mastiff is one of the bigger mastiff breeds.

DOG DATA!

In 2014 a buyer paid $1.9 million for a Tibetan Mastiff puppy.

From Tibet to the States

Two mastiffs arrived in the United States from Tibet in the 1950s, but little is known of them. The breed did not really take off until the 1970s, when several more were imported from India and Nepal. Decades of breeding have made the Tibetan Mastiff less aggressive, but it is still a good guard dog.

The black-and-tan Tibetan Mastiff has tan "eyebrows," and a thick, black mane.

SUPER SCHNAUZERS

From the 15th century, farmers in the Munich area of Germany were using the Giant Schnauzer to drive cattle. When the railways arrived, cattle trains meant the breed fell out of favor. Today, though, it is more popular than ever.

BREED PROFILE

NAME: **Giant Schnauzer**

ORIGIN: **Germany**

COLORS: **Black, and salt-and-pepper**

EYE COLORS: **Dark brown**

WEIGHT RANGE: **65–90 lb**

LIFE EXPECTANCY: **12 years**

CHARACTER: **Trainable, energetic, and lovable**

The Miniature Schnauzer comes in a range of appealing colors, including white.

All-Around Performer

The Giant Schnauzer was developed from the Standard Schnauzer, which was a perfect all-around farm dog. It could drive cattle, herd sheep, guard homes and stables, and even pull a small cart to market. The breed also made a good-looking pet. The 15th-century German painter Albrecht Dürer and the 17th-century Dutch painter Rembrandt both owned Standard Schnauzers.

The Standard Schnauzer weighs up to 44 pounds.

The Giant Schnauzer's dense, wiry coat can be solid black, like here, or flecked with white (salt-and-pepper).

Huge Personality

Like its larger cousins, the Miniature Schnauzer was also developed in Germany. Intelligent and energetic, it was first used as a ratting dog. It stands just 14 inches tall at the shoulder.

DOG DATA!

The breed name comes from the German word Schnauze, meaning "snout."

85

SPECIAL SPANIELS

Spaniel simply means "dog from Spain." Two of the most popular breeds are the American and English Cocker Spaniels, once considered the same breed but recognized as separate breeds since 1946. The American Cocker is in the Top 15 of popular dog breeds.

Cockers and Springers

The Springer Spaniel was the founder of all English Spaniel breeds. It was used to flush out game from cover and named for its habit of startling birds into the air by springing! Originally the Cocker was not a separate breed. The smallest Springer puppies in a litter were used for hunting small game birds called woodcock.

The Springer Spaniel often has freckling around the nose and on the legs.

Good Gundog

Thought to have originated in France more than 200 years ago, the first Clumber Spaniel was brought to England by the Duke of Newcastle, and bred at his family home, Clumber Park. It is bigger and heavier than other Spaniel breeds, but makes a good gundog. Not a natural swimmer, it will go into water to retrieve game and its thick coat keeps it warm.

The Clumber Spaniel has a broader, deeper muzzle than other Spaniel breeds.

This American Cocker has a "show coat." Working dogs have their legs shaved.

BREED PROFILE

NAME: **American Cocker**

ORIGIN: **United States**

COLORS: **All colors**

EYE COLORS: **Dark brown and blue**

WEIGHT RANGE: **15–30 lb**

LIFE EXPECTANCY: **15 years**

CHARACTER: **Active, cheerful, and sweet-tempered**

BEAUTIFUL BASSETS

Bassets are sniffer dogs that hunt low to the ground—the name comes from the French word *bas*, meaning "low." Medieval French monks are said to have bred the first Bassets for hunting rabbits and hares. Today there are six recognized breeds.

Large and Small

The Basset Griffon Vendéen comes from the Vendée area of western France. There are two sizes: Grand and Petit (large and small). Both types are outgoing, smart, and make charming family pets.

This Grand Basset Griffon Vendéen has a white coat with orange markings.

Blue by Name

Like all the Basset family, the Bleu de Gascogne is short in stature, but long in personality. It almost became extinct in the 1900s, but was rescued by crossbreeding with the larger Bleu de Gascogne Hound. The distinctive black-mottled coat on a white base gives it a "blue" color.

Despite its sad-looking eyes, the Basset Hound is a good-natured dog that makes a fine pet.

The Basset Bleu de Gascogne is not speedy but it is determined and will track its quarry for hours.

BREED PROFILE

NAME: **Basset Hound**

ORIGIN: **England, UK**

COLORS: **Black and white, tan and white, and tricolor**

EYE COLORS: **Dark brown and blue**

WEIGHT RANGE: **40–60 lb**

LIFE EXPECTANCY: **14 years**

CHARACTER: **Loving, playful, and loyal**

89

ON THE SCENT

The Basset is just one type of scenthound—many other breeds were originally developed to assist hunters with their powerful senses of smell. The Beagle is one of the best-known. Unlike the Foxhound, which accompanied horseback hunters, it typically hunted with people on foot.

Pack Animal

The Foxhound was used in England to hunt foxes for more than 300 years. In the United States, it is more likely to run down coyotes than foxes. Happiest as a pack animal, the Foxhound is rarely kept successfully as a household pet.

Foxhounds make a noisy baying sound when they bark.

Saint Hubert's Hound

Distinguished by its wrinkly skin and drooping ears, the Bloodhound was developed by Belgian monks at the Monastery of Saint Hubert more than 1,000 years ago. Its spectacular sniffing power has made it a popular choice as a police sniffer dog.

The Bloodhound has distinctive droopy ears.

The Otterhound is very easygoing. It still has a strong hunting instinct.

Hunting Otter

As its name suggests, the Otterhound was used to hunt otters in Britain's rivers, until the sport was banned in the 1970s. Today, the breed is extremely rare. The Otterhound is a big, strong dog with a shaggy double coat, and it is an excellent swimmer.

The Beagle hunts rabbits and hares.

BREED PROFILE

NAME: **Beagle**

ORIGIN: **England, UK**

COLORS: **Yellow and white, tan and white, and black and tan**

EYE COLORS: **Brown**

WEIGHT RANGE: **Up to 70 lb**

LIFE EXPECTANCY: **10 years**

CHARACTER: **Brave, intelligent, and friendly**

COONHOUNDS

Coonhounds are all-American scent hounds used to track raccoons as well as opossums, deer, cougars, and bears. They are based on the English Foxhound and Bloodhound with perhaps a dash of Kerry Beagle and Bleu de Gascogne in the mix.

DOG DATA!

North Carolina's state dog, the Plott Hound, is a type of Coonhound. It has a brindled coat.

The Treeing Walker Coonhound is one of the fastest Coonhound breeds.

In adulthood, this Redbone Coonhound puppy's fur will darken and gleam.

Treeing Prey

Coonhounds are good at tracking prey and do not give up when it runs up a tree—they simply wait and bark to alert the hunter. This method of cornering prey up a tree is called "treeing." The Coonhound's distinctive deep howl, known as a bay, is a reminder of its Foxhound heritage.

Colored Coats

Some Coonhound breeds are named for their coloring. The Black-and-Tan Coonhound is mostly coal-black, with a tan muzzle and "shoes;" the Bluetick Coonhound is ticked blue-gray; and the Redbone Coonhound has a solid red coat.

Ticked Three Ways

The most popular breed today for raccoon hunting is the American-English Coonhound, which may have a redtick, bluetick, or tricolored tick coat. It is descended from hounds brought to America during the 17th and 18th centuries.

Redtick is the most common color for the American-English Coonhound.

BREED PROFILE

NAME: **Black-and-Tan Coonhound**

ORIGIN: **United States**

COLORS: **Black-and-tan**

EYE COLORS: **Dark brown**

WEIGHT RANGE: **50–75 lb**

LIFE EXPECTANCY: **12 years**

CHARACTER: **Playful, loving, and independent**

The Black-and-Tan Coonhound raises its tail like this when it is on a scent trail.

WATER DOGS

Water dogs are at home in the water. They have been bred to **flush out** waterfowl or to retrieve fishermen's nets—or both! These are all adaptable working dogs and they have curled or corded coats that are designed to repel water.

Fishermen used the Portuguese Water Dog to retrieve dropped tackle. It would swim from boat to boat.

The Spanish Water Dog's coat can be sheared like a sheep's.

Black Beauty

The earliest mention of a Portuguese Water Dog describes one saving a drowning man and dates to 1297. The dog had a "black coat, long and rough, cut to the first rib, and with a tuft on the tip of his tail." Traders from North Africa probably brought the Portuguese Water Dog to Portugal.

All-Purpose Animal

Portugal's neighbor country, Spain, has its own breed of water dog. The Spanish Water Dog loves to swim, but it will also happily herd sheep or goats, or act as a guard dog.

State Spaniel

The American Water Spaniel was developed in Wisconsin, where it is the official state dog, to work out of skiffs (small river boats) and retrieve from icy rivers and lakes. It was smaller than the retrievers of the time, but hardy enough to swim for long periods.

As a pet, the American Water Spaniel is best suited to families with a very active lifestyle.

This is a liver-colored American Water Spaniel; the breed can also be chocolate. Both colors may have white hairs.

DOG DATA!

In the 1960s, the Portuguese Water Dog was listed in the *Guinness Book of Records* as the rarest pedigree breed.

GENTLE GIANTS

No other animal comes in such an incredible range of sizes as the domestic dog. In terms of height, the Great Dane is the largest of them all. It was originally bred to hunt wild boar and bears and is a very old breed—ancient Greek coins dating back to 36 BCE feature a dog that looks like a Great Dane.

The Rottweiler is always black with red markings over the eyes, on the cheeks, muzzle, chest, and legs,and beneath the tail

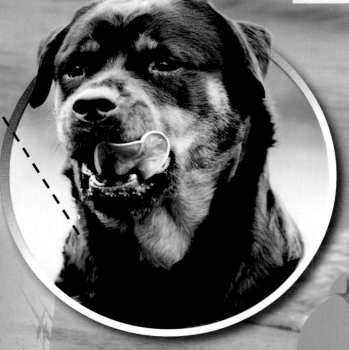

Guardians of Cattle

The Rottweiler is named for the German city of Rottweil, where it was used to protect cattle from predators and thieves. This strong and powerful dog is probably descended from Italian Mastiffs brought to the region during the time of the Roman Empire.

DOG DATA!

The tallest dog was a Great Dane called Zeus who measured 44 inches high.

The Deerhound's coat is usually a blue-gray color.

The Deer Hunter

Although it is skinnier than the Great Dane, the Deerhound can stand just as tall—up to 30 inches at the shoulder. The Deerhound was already in Scotland more than 2,000 years ago. It was used for red deer **coursing**. Hounds were let off the leash one at a time or in pairs and either brought down deer or cornered them until the hunter arrived.

The black Great Dane sometimes has white markings on its chest.

NEWFOUNDLAND

Mystery surrounds the origins of the Newfoundland. Although the First Nation People who lived on the Canadian island of Newfoundland had dogs, they bore no resemblance to the modern Newfoundland. The dog looks much like the Tibetan Mastiff, with its massive size and thick, heavy coat.

DOG DATA!

In 1919 a Newfoundland called Tang saved the 92 crew of a ship that had run aground. It swam to shore with the ship's rope.

Canadian Cousin

The Newfoundland shares some characteristics with the Labrador (see pages 68–69), which was once known as the Lesser Newfoundland Dog. These include its water-resistant coat, webbed feet, and rudder-like tail. The breed has become larger and sturdier over time.

The Newfoundland's thick double coat needs brushing at least two or three times a week.

Shipwrecked Victims

During the 19th century, Newfoundland dogs were being used along the coasts of Canada, the United States, and England. Some worked as lifeguards to rescue swimmers. Others accompanied fishermen on their boats, hauling in nets, carrying boat lines to shore, and retrieving anything that fell overboard. Its reputation for rescuing shipwrecked or drowning victims earned it the nickname "Saint Bernard of the Water."

Newfoundlands are strong swimmers, but rescue ones wear life jackets for safety.

Newfoundlands with a black-and-white coat are called Landseer Newfoundlands. In some places, the Landseer is considered a separate breed.

BREED PROFILE

NAME: **Newfoundland**

ORIGIN: **Canada**

COLORS: **Black, brown, and Landseer (black-and-white)**

EYE COLORS: **Dark brown**

WEIGHT RANGE: **Up to 150 lb**

LIFE EXPECTANCY: **10 years**

CHARACTER: **Gentle, intelligent, and playful**

PERFECT POODLES

Poodles originally came from Germany, where they were bred as a type of water dog. However, they are more associated with the neighboring country of France, where the different sizes developed. The Standard Poodle, known as the *Caniche* ("duck dog"), was a water dog; smaller ones were used to sniff out truffles.

Square Dogs

The Miniature and Toy Poodles developed in the 18th century, when there was a fashion for small companion dogs. Whatever the size, a Poodle should be "square"—in other words, its height should equal its length.

Some Toy Poodles are therapy dogs in nursing homes. They are gentle and love to be petted.

This Toy Poodle has a solid red coat.

Corded Poodle

All Poodles' coats will form twisted cords if they are allowed to grow long. The Corded Poodle has been specially bred for this feature, although it is not recognized as a separate breed from the Standard.

Corded Poodles are very rare. Their coats take a very long time to dry after washing.

DOG DATA!

The German name for the Poodle is *Pudelhund*, meaning "dog that splashes about."

With the Poodle Clip, fluffy pom-poms are left on all four ankles.

Practical Style

A natural clown, the Poodle performed in French circuses. However, its distinctive "Poodle Clip" was developed not for entertainment but for practicality. Removing the thick hair around the middle of the body made the dog lighter in the water, and prevented snagging. Leaving hair on the leg joints protected them from icy water and sharp reeds.

MOUNTAIN DOGS

Dogs that work in the mountains need strong legs for climbing and thick fur to insulate against the cold. They usually have broad chests housing powerful lungs, too, so they can take in as much oxygen as possible from the high-altitude air.

The handsome Bernese Mountain Dog has a white cross on its chest.

DOG DATA!

The Bernese Mountain Dog is still sometimes used to pull carts.

Alpine Shepherd

The famous Saint Bernard is closely related to the tricolored cattle dogs that work in the Swiss Alps—the Bernese Mountain Dog, Greater Swiss Mountain Dog, Appenzeller, and Entlebucher. Of these, the Bernese is the only one with long hair. It is large and well-built, but has a sweet and gentle nature, and is especially good with children.

Cattle Dog

The Appenzeller is one of the smaller Swiss mountain dogs. Like the others, it has a black, tan, and white coat. It originated in northeastern Switzerland, where it was used to herd and guard cattle.

The Appenzeller is named after the Appenzell Alps, a mountain range on the northern edge of the Swiss Alps.

The Saint Bernard was bred as a rescue dog in the Swiss Alps.

Portuguese Protector

The Estrela Mountain Dog is large and sturdy. Farmers in the Estrela Mountains of northern Portugal used it to guard their flocks of sheep and goats. It traditionally wore a spiked metal collar to protect it from a wolf attack.

The Estrela Mountain Dog can be fawn, gray, or yellow. It weighs up to 110 pounds.

PYRENEAN MOUNTAIN DOG

In its native France, the Pyrenean Mountain Dog is known as the *Grande Pyrenees*. It was traditionally a herder's dog, used to protect flocks from wolves and bears. It is related to the Saint Bernard (see pages 102–103) and the Hungarian Kuvasz (see page 58).

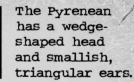

The Pyrenean has a wedge-shaped head and smallish, triangular ears.

Super Snowshoes

The Pyrenean Mountain Dog was suited to its home ground, the Pyrenees Mountains on the border between France and Spain. Conditions could be harsh high in the mountains, but the Pyrenean's thick, double coat kept it warm. It also has unusual double dew claws on its hind feet that act as "snowshoes," giving it grip in deep snow.

DOG DATA!

In 1675, Louis XIV of France named the Pyrenean the "Royal Dog of France."

BREED PROFILE

NAME: **Pyrenean Mountain Dog**

ORIGIN: **France**

COLORS: **Mostly white**

EYE COLORS: **Dark brown**

WEIGHT RANGE: **88–110 lb**

LIFE EXPECTANCY: **12 years**

CHARACTER: **Laid-back, friendly, and calm**

The Pyrenean's thick coat can be solid white, or have patches of gray, tan, or yellow.

The Protector

Strong, brave, and intelligent, the Pyrenean is still used as a working sheepdog and guard dog. However, its easygoing nature also makes it an excellent pet. In spite of its huge size, the breed does not require enormous amounts of exercise.

A working Pyrenean is very protective of its flock.

SHEPHERD DOGS

Developed to look after farmers' flocks of sheep, sheepdogs have qualities that make them highly valued as pets and in other working dog roles. The most famous sheepdog is the German Shepherd, which was developed by a German cavalry captain at the end of the 19th century.

Long fur covers the face and eyes of the Old English Sheepdog.

One Breed

There were once thought to be two breeds of Italian sheepdog, the Maremmano and the Abruzzese, both with a magnificent white coat. The Abruzzese was more of a mountain dog, with a longer body and thicker coat. Today, they are considered to be the same breed, known simply as the Maremma.

The Maremma is a large dog, weighing up to 100 pounds.

Bobtailed Breed

The Old English Sheepdog was used to herd sheep and drive cattle. Farmers **docked** their dogs' tails to identify them as working dogs, which meant they paid less tax. For this reason, the breed was sometimes known as the Bobtail Sheepdog. Mostly white on its head and chest, its shaggy coat is gray, grizzle, or blue on the body and hindquarters.

Obedient and with an excellent sense of smell, the German Shepherd is used by police and armies all over the world.

BREED PROFILE

NAME: **German Shepherd Dog**

ORIGIN: **Germany**

COLORS: **Black, tan, bicolor, and sable**

EYE COLORS: **Dark brown and blue**

WEIGHT RANGE: **22–40 lb**

LIFE EXPECTANCY: **10 years**

CHARACTER: **Intelligent, versatile, and strong**

LOVABLE COLLIES

Collies are intelligent herding dogs that have boundless energy and need a lot of exercise. Many are still used as working sheepdogs; some are trained to take part in agility competitions. Their name comes from *col*, the Anglo-Saxon word for "black."

Thanks to its sleek coat, the Smooth Collie is easier to maintain than the Rough Collie.

Rough and Smooth

The Rough Collie and Smooth Collie are counted as the same breed in the United States, just with different coat lengths. Elsewhere, they are sometimes considered two separate breeds. Both have been used by Scottish shepherds for centuries. The breed became popular after Queen Victoria introduced them to the royal kennels, following a visit to Scotland in 1860.

DOG DATA!

The famous film star Lassie was a Rough Collie—but "she" was played by a male dog!

Life on the Edge

The Border Collie is another herding dog, named because it was used by shepherds on the hills along the border counties of England, Scotland, and Wales. It was bred for its boundless energy—some days, it was required to run more than 50 miles!

The Border Collie is famous for being one of the most intelligent and trainable breeds of dog.

The Rough Collie has a fluffy white mane and feathering on its tail and hind legs.

BREED PROFILE

NAME: **Rough Collie**

ORIGIN: **Scotland, UK**

COLORS: **Black, tan, and white, or blue merle**

EYE COLORS: **Dark brown**

WEIGHT RANGE: **50–75 lb**

LIFE EXPECTANCY: **14 years**

CHARACTER: **Intelligent, loyal, and energetic**

LION DOGS

Lion Dog is the perfect nickname for dogs with an impressive mane, such as the Pekingese and Löwchen, which are both companion dogs. The Rhodesian Ridgeback is a bigger beast altogether but it, too, has a **leonine** hairstyle.

Luxury Lion

The Pekingese comes from China, where it was held in such high regard that only the emperor or members of his family were allowed to own one. It existed as long ago as the Tang Dynasty (618–907 CE) and is one of the earliest examples of a lap dog, standing no more than 9 inches at the shoulder.

Like the Poodle, the Löwchen is often given an elaborate hairstyle, with the coat clipped at the back and left long at the front.

The tiny Pekingese has a long mane surrounding its short-muzzled face.

Little Lion Dog

The Löwchen developed in France or Germany more than 400 years ago. Its name, which means "Little Lion Dog" in German, refers to the ruff of fur around its neck. The breed is related to the Poodle (see pages 100–101) and Bichon Frise (see page 114).

110

The Lion Hunter

Also known as the African Lion Hound, the Rhodesian Ridgeback was developed in Rhodesia (now Zimbabwe) to hunt big game such as lions. It is a large and powerful dog; males can weigh up to 90 pounds.

The Rhodesian Ridgeback is named for the long line of raised hair that runs along its back.

The Pekingese was named after the Chinese capital, Peking (now known as Beijing).

DOG DATA!

According to Chinese legend, the Pekingese was the result of a lion falling in love with a marmoset (tiny monkey).

HARD WORKERS

Some companion dogs are smaller versions of larger working breeds. However, some larger dogs are also grouped with the companion dogs, because they rarely have to earn their keep or do a job.

This museum exhibit shows a model Dalmatian in the firehouse.

DOG DATA!

The longest tongue on a dog according to the Guinness Book of Records belonged to a Boxer called Brandy—17 inches!

Former Farm Dog

The German word *Pinscher* means "terrier," but the German Pinscher is much taller than a terrier, with longer legs. Traditionally used on farms to catch rats, herd livestock, and be a watchdog, these days it leads a pampered life.

Firehouse Dog

The Dalmatian is kept only as a pet these days, but in the past it was used to guard property, pull carriages, and entertain in the circus. In the 19th century, firefighters had the dog run ahead of their horse-drawn fire engines. When people saw the spotted "firehouse dog," they knew to get out of the way.

The German Pinscher's ears prick up when it is alert.

Smart Companion

Patient and protective, the Boxer is consistently one of the Top Ten most popular dog breeds in the United States. However, it was originally bred for dog fights and **bull-baiting**, as well as to hunt large animals, such as wild boar.

The Boxer is a highly intelligent dog. Today it is still used for rescue work and as a guard dog.

BREED PROFILE

NAME: **Boxer**

ORIGIN: **Germany**

COLORS: **Brown or brindle**

EYE COLORS: **Dark brown**

WEIGHT RANGE: **60–105 lb**

LIFE EXPECTANCY: **12 years**

CHARACTER: **Loyal, brave, and active**

FABULOUS AND FLUFFY

A favorite feature of lap dogs is a coat that is delightful to touch. Some owners prefer soft and silky breeds, but others want extreme fluffiness! The Lhasa Apso is one of the fluffiest of them all.

Fluff Ball

The Bichon Frise may look like a ball of white cotton candy, but its full coat does not make a mess because it is non-shedding. It is sometimes called the Tenerife dog because French sailors are said to have discovered the breed on the island of Tenerife in the Atlantic.

DOG DATA!

The Lhasa Apso was originally kept as a guard dog in Tibetan palaces and monasteries.

The Bichon Frise is always white, with dramatic dark eyes.

Hair over the Lhasa Apso's eyes protects them from wind, sand, and glare.

Hairy Chin

Weighing less than 7 pounds, the Japanese Chin has a long, silky coat and a feathered tail. It makes a sweet-natured companion dog. It is said to be descended from a dog given as a gift from China to the Emperor of Japan.

The Japanese Chin has the same short muzzle as the Pekingese (see page 110).

BREED PROFILE

NAME: Lhasa Apso

ORIGIN: Tibet, China

COLORS: Honey, black, white, slate, and parti-color

EYE COLORS: Brown

WEIGHT RANGE: 44–66 lb

LIFE EXPECTANCY: 15 years

CHARACTER: Happy, playful, and independent

COZY COATS

Thick, bushy coats are an important feature for dogs from cold parts of the world. Most have a double coat: a dense undercoat for insulation topped with a harsher outer coat to repel snow and rain. The Chow Chow's outer coat can be rough or smooth—both are delightful to pet.

NAME: Chow Chow

ORIGIN: China

COLORS: Red, black, blue, cinnamon, and cream

EYE COLORS: Brown, blue, and amber

WEIGHT RANGE: 45–75 lb

LIFE EXPECTANCY: 15 years

CHARACTER: Intelligent, brave, and loyal

China's Chow

Along with its thick coat, the Chow Chow is also known for its unique, bluish-black tongue. The breed was used as a guard dog and for hunting in China for more than 2,000 years, but only reached the wider world in the 19th century.

According to legend, the Chow Chow got its blue coloring by licking the sky when it was being painted.

DOG DATA!

There are only four recognized colors of the Japanese Akita Inu.

116

Red is the most popular coat color for the Chow Chow. This is the rough-coated version.

Polar Dog

The most popular dog breed in Japan, the Akita Inu arrived in the northern mountains of Japan from the polar regions thousands of years ago. Only the biggest and strongest were used for breeding, resulting in the modern Akita breed.

Akita Inu means "large dog," but really the breed is medium-sized. An Akita Inu weighs up to 55 pounds and stands 25 inches at the shoulder.

Viking Breed

Dogs found in graves in the Scandinavian countries of Denmark and Sweden from around 5000 BCE share many common traits with the Icelandic Sheepdog. As Norwegian Vikings sailed to Iceland in 874 CE, they took their dogs with them. It has been illegal to bring animals into Iceland since 1901.

Like a typical Spitz (see pages 120–121), the Icelandic Sheepdog holds its tail curled over its back.

SLED DOGS

Before the days of snowmobiles, sled was the only way to travel in the snowbound north. Many dog breeds were used to pull sleds, including the Alaskan Malamute, Siberian Husky, Samoyed, and Canadian Eskimo Dog.

BREED PROFILE

NAME: **Alaskan Malamute**

ORIGIN: **United States**

COLORS: **White, gray, black, sable, and red**

EYE COLORS: **Brown**

WEIGHT RANGE: **90–110 lb**

LIFE EXPECTANCY: **15 years**

CHARACTER: **Playful, friendly, and sociable**

Canine Heater

The fastest of all the sled-pulling dogs, the Husky comes from northeastern Siberia, in Russia. The nomadic Chukchi people used them to haul their sleds and guard them at night. Children often slept cuddled up to a Husky for warmth. Huskies are known for their amazing endurance.

The Husky is one of the few dog breeds to have piercing blue eyes.

Reindeer Herder

The Samoyedic people of northern Siberia kept a different Arctic hound—the beautiful Samoyed. Its thick, white coat made it hard to spot against the snowy landscape. The Samoyed herded and guarded reindeer and pulled sleds. It even provided people with clothing—they made yarn out of the fur that it shed.

The Samoyed has a soft white coat with silver-tipped outer hairs.

DOG DATA!

In 1925, Siberian Huskies saved the children of Nome, Alaska, from an epidemic by helping to bring medicine to the town.

The Malamute is named for Alaska's indigenous people. They are known as the Kobuk, but the first Western settlers called them the Mahlemut.

STURDY SPITZES

The German Spitz comes in two sizes: Klein (small) and Mittel (standard). Both are descended from the herding dogs used by people in the Arctic. Confusingly, the Pomeranian, which is descended from the German Spitz, looks almost exactly the same as the German Spitz Klein!

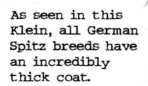

As seen in this Klein, all German Spitz breeds have an incredibly thick coat.

Tiny Klein

Both German Spitz sizes are considered to be the same breed. The Mittel stands up to 15 inches at the shoulder, while the Klein can be no more than 11.5 inches. The **FCI** recognizes a third size within the breed, too: the Gross (giant), which can be up to 20 inches at the shoulder.

BREED PROFILE

NAME: **German Spitz (Klein)**

ORIGIN: **Germany**

COLORS: **Black, brown, orange, wolf-gray, and white**

EYE COLORS: **Dark brown**

WEIGHT RANGE: **18–22 lb**

LIFE EXPECTANCY: **15 years**

CHARACTER: **Happy, alert, and bold**

The Pomeranian is an alert little dog, and surprisingly fast.

Noisy Hunter

In its native Finland, the Finnish Spitz is known as the "Finnish pricked ear dog." It has small, pointed ears and a fox-like face and coat. Traditionally used as a hunting dog, it has a surprisingly loud bark for alerting its owner when it finds game.

The Finnish Spitz is Finland's national dog.

DOG DATA!

The Finnish Spitz can bark more than 160 times a minute.

The Japanese Spitz's coat is always long, lustrous, and pure white.

White and Handsome

The exact origins of the Japanese Spitz are unknown, but with its long, white coat and bushy tail, it looks like a smaller version of the Samoyed. It is now popular around the world, not just in its native Japan.

MERRY TERRIERS

Terriers take their name from the Latin word *terra*, meaning earth. The first ones were small dogs bred to hunt down underground vermin such as rats. In the 19th century, a new kind of terrier became popular, by crossing terriers with bulldogs. These bull terriers were used for **pit-fighting**.

BREED PROFILE

NAME: American Staffordshire Terrier

ORIGIN: United States

COLORS: Solid color, patched, and parti

EYE COLORS: Brown

WEIGHT RANGE: 55–65 lb

LIFE EXPECTANCY: 10–16 years

CHARACTER: Gentle, loving, and loyal

One of the First Terriers

The Fox Terrier dates back to the 17th century, when it was developed in England by crossing Dachshunds with Foxhounds and Beagles. Farmers used the Fox Terrier to keep down pests such as rats and foxes, which ate valuable feed or livestock and carried disease.

The classic Fox Terrier is wire-haired, but there is also a smooth-coated version.

The Cesky Terrier's long facial hair forms a "beard."

Bohemian Ratter

The stocky Cesky Terrier is a fairly new breed, developed in the Czech Republic using Sealyham (see page 124) and Scottish Terrier breeds. It is a tough and fearless ratter, able to enter narrow burrows after its prey. It is also known as the Bohemian or Czech Terrier.

The American Staffordshire Terrier developed from the Staffordshire Bull Terrier. It is a sturdy, agile dog, with an outgoing personality.

123

BRITISH TERRIERS

Many terrier breeds originated in the United Kingdom, including the largest one, the Airedale Terrier. It was bred in Yorkshire, England, to hunt otters and rats in the area between the Aire, Calder, and Wharfe Rivers, and is nicknamed the "king of terriers."

Sparky Sealyham

Captain John Tucker Edwards developed the Sealyham in the 19th century at his country estate in Wales. The sparky little dog was used to go after badgers and otters. These days it is kept only as a pet, not a working dog.

The Sealyham stands up to 12 inches at the shoulder.

BREED PROFILE

NAME: **Airedale Terrier**

ORIGIN: **England, UK**

COLORS: **Black and tan, grizzled (gray and black) and tan, red speckling**

EYE COLORS: **Brown**

WEIGHT RANGE: **40–64 lb**

LIFE EXPECTANCY: **10 years**

CHARACTER: **Brave, happy, and confident**

The Airedale Terrier is an upright, stocky dog with a beared muzzle.

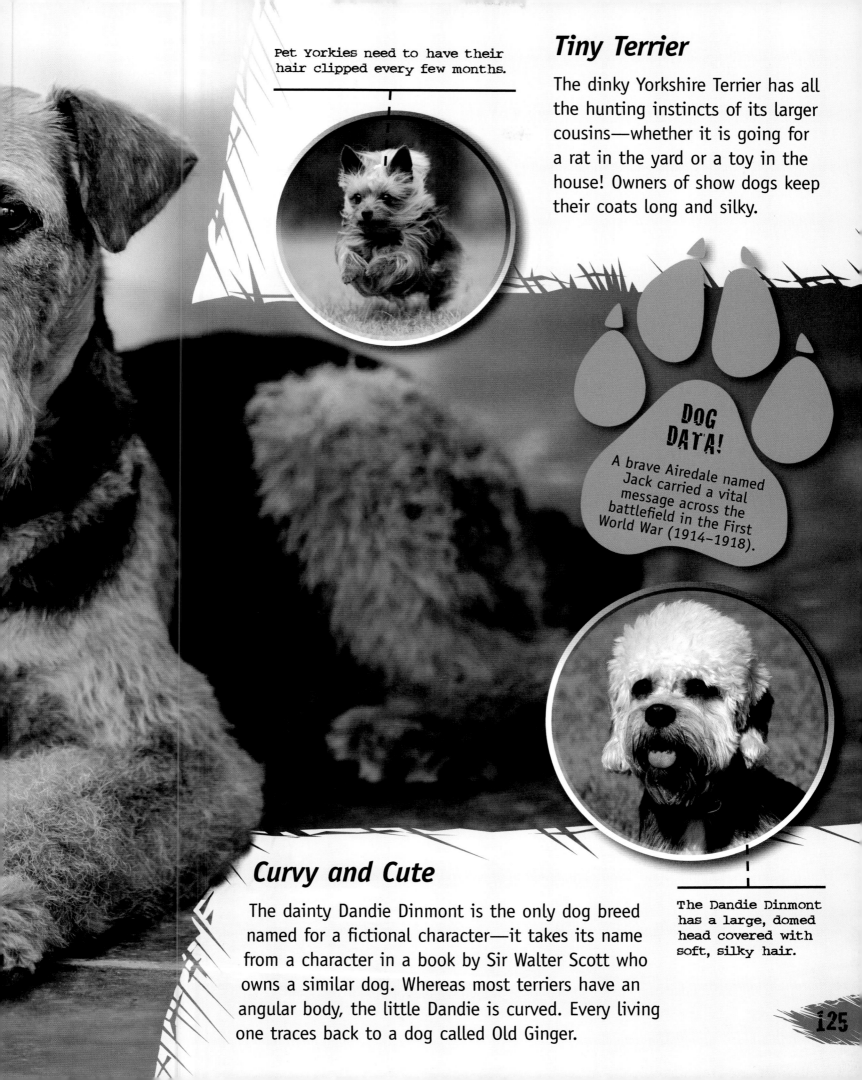

Pet Yorkies need to have their hair clipped every few months.

Tiny Terrier

The dinky Yorkshire Terrier has all the hunting instincts of its larger cousins—whether it is going for a rat in the yard or a toy in the house! Owners of show dogs keep their coats long and silky.

DOG DATA!

A brave Airedale named Jack carried a vital message across the battlefield in the First World War (1914–1918).

Curvy and Cute

The dainty Dandie Dinmont is the only dog breed named for a fictional character—it takes its name from a character in a book by Sir Walter Scott who owns a similar dog. Whereas most terriers have an angular body, the little Dandie is curved. Every living one traces back to a dog called Old Ginger.

The Dandie Dinmont has a large, domed head covered with soft, silky hair.

JACK RUSSELL TERRIER

The Reverend John "Jack" Russell developed the breed that bears his name as a working terrier in Oxford, England, in the early 19th century. He used it to dig out foxes that had gone to ground (burrowed into the earth).

DOG DATA!

The Jack Russell breed began with an almost-white little dog called Trump.

Working Terrier

The original Jack Russell was bred to be small enough to get into foxes' dens, but long-legged enough to keep up with horseriders and hounds on the hunt. Today, there are two separate breeds: the Jack Russell is the working type and has the shorter legs. It stands no more than 12 inches at the shoulder.

All Jack Russells make playful and affectionate pets.

The Jack Russell can be wire-haired (as here) or smooth-haired (left).

Made for Show

Today, the longer-legged breed is known as the Parson Russell Terrier—this is the breed that was accepted as a pedigree by the AKC in 2012, becoming the AKC's 175th breed. The Parson Russell is more of a show dog and has a stricter **breed standard** than the working type of terrier.

The energetic Parson Russell Terrier needs plenty of exercise.

BREED PROFILE

NAME: **Jack Russell Terrier**

ORIGIN: **England, UK**

COLORS: **White with black, tan, or brindle markings**

EYE COLORS: **Brown**

WEIGHT RANGE: **11–13 lb**

LIFE EXPECTANCY: **15 years or more**

CHARACTER: **Brave, lively, and intelligent**

PERFECT POINTERS

Two kinds of gundog locate prey; setters (see pages 72–73) and **pointers**. A pointer's special talent is to freeze and "point" its nose, body, and tail in the direction of prey, such as a rabbit or bird.

Three Coats

Today there are three recognized German Pointers: long-haired, wire-haired, and short-haired. The longhair is the largest, but the shorthair is the most common. All three are good at tracking, pointing, and retrieving.

The German Short-Haired Pointer began by crossing Schweisshunds—slow hounds that had talent for scenting game—with English Pointers.

DOG DATA!

The Portuguese Pointing Dog was recognized as a breed in 2013.

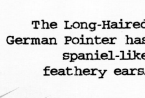

The Long-Haired German Pointer has spaniel-like feathery ears.

Partridge Dog

The Portuguese Pointing Dog can be seen in hunting scenes painted as early as the 14th century. It was bred to locate partridges for huntsmen using falcons and nets. Although it looks like a cross between a yellow Labrador and a Boxer, the Portuguese Pointing Dog is a pure breed in its own right.

The breed's Portuguese name translates as "Portuguese Partridge Dog."

BREED PROFILE

NAME: **German Pointer**

ORIGIN: **Germany**

COLORS: **Black, liver, and ticked**

EYE COLORS: **Brown**

WEIGHT RANGE: **44–71 lb**

LIFE EXPECTANCY: **15 years**

CHARACTER: **Willing, friendly, and alert**

The Slovakian Rough-Haired Pointer has a sable coat and amber eyes.

Hunting Instinct

The Slovakian Rough-Haired Pointer is thought to be a cross between a Weimaraner and a German Wire-Haired Pointer. It has the hunting instinct and scenting abilities of both.

ALL ABOUT HAIR

The Corded Poodle (see page 101) is not the only breed that can develop dreadlocks. Two dogs originating in Hungary exhibit the same characteristic. Their coats are hard to care for, but completely unforgettable.

Large and Small

The tight, corded curls of the Hungarian Puli's coat keep the rain out and the dog warm. When the Magyar tribes swept into Europe from Asia 1,200 years ago, they brought tough, long-coated herding dogs like the modern Puli.

Each cord of the Hungarian Puli's thick, tasseled coat feels like felt.

The Hungarian Puli is energetic. It needs plenty of fun and company.

DOG DATA!

It takes four to five years for the Hungarian Puli's coat to form its cords.

The Komondor's corded coat comes only in one color: white.

BREED PROFILE

NAME: **Hungarian Puli**

ORIGIN: **Hungary**

COLORS: **White, gray, fawn, and black**

EYE COLORS: **Dark brown**

WEIGHT RANGE: **22–33 lb**

LIFE EXPECTANCY: **12 years**

CHARACTER: **Smart, eager to please, and loyal**

Big Barker

At first glance, the Komondor looks much like the Hungarian Puli. The breeds may share the same homeland and both have a corded coat, but they are very different. The Komondor is nearly twice as tall and four times as heavy as the Puli! Big and strong, it has a ferocious bark and was used to guard livestock.

131

MARVELOUS MIXES

Besides all the pedigree breeds of dog, there are crossbreeds. Some are random, never to be repeated. Others are created on purpose to combine characteristics from two different breeds. The names of these crossbreeds often reveal their parent breeds.

Popular and Playful

Like many crossbreeds, the Labradoodle was not created to be a designer dog, but for practical reasons. It has a lower risk of inherited diseases than its parent dogs, the Labrador and Poodle. It makes a wonderful gundog, assistance animal, or family pet. A similar cross is the Goldendoodle, which is half-Golden Retriever and half-Poodle.

The Goldendoodle has been around since the early 1980s. Its coat can be straight, wavy, or curly.

The Labradoodle comes in three sizes: Miniature, Medium, and Standard.

BREED PROFILE

NAME: **Standard Labradoodle**

ORIGIN: **Australia**

COLORS: **All**

EYE COLORS: **Brown or ghost (hazel)**

WEIGHT RANGE: **50–65 lb**

LIFE EXPECTANCY: **15 years**

CHARACTER: **Intelligent, playful, and friendly**

The Standard Cockapoo weighs around 22 pounds.

More Poodle Crosses

The Cockapoo, a mix of American or English Cocker Spaniel with a Toy, Miniature, or Standard Poodle, makes a charming, friendly dog. Cockapoos love playing and learning new tricks. Another favorite, the Yorkipoo is part-Poodle (Toy or Miniature), part-Yorkshire Terrier—and a natural show-off!

133

FROM PUPPY TO DOG

Everything is new and exciting to young puppies like these Golden Retrievers.

Smaller dog breeds usually have litters of one to four puppies, while bigger dogs have larger litters. The Labrador Retriever's average litter size is between seven and eight. Whatever the number of puppies, newborns are completely dependent on their mother for the first couple of weeks of life.

Early Development

At around two weeks, the puppies' eyes and ears open and they can see and hear. They learn to stand, toddle, and walk. Their teeth come through, so they begin to eat solid food as well as feed on mother's milk. The puppies can wag their tails and bark.

DOG DATA!

The record for the largest litter of puppies is 24, delivered by a Neapolitan Mastiff called Tia in 2009.

Newborn puppies only wake up to feed. They spend the rest of the time sleeping.

Adventurous Play

By five weeks old, puppies have been weaned and are aware of their surroundings. The puppies enjoy roughhousing with each other and become more independent. However, they must stay with their mother until they are at least eight weeks old.

Play helps the puppies develop the skills that they will need as adults.

A New Home

Toilet training usually begins by week seven, and other basic training (see pages 138–139) by eight weeks. The puppy usually leaves its mother and littermates and goes to live with a new owner. It soon learns its place in this new "pack" or family.

A new owner accustoms her King Charles Spaniel puppy to being on the leash.

135

DOG CARE

A dog is totally dependent on its owner, so the owner must meet its basic needs. One of the biggest responsibilities is giving the dog enough exercise. Depending on the breed, a twice-daily walk of at least 30 minutes—and sometimes much more—will be vital to their well-being.

DOG DATA!

Chocolate may seem like a treat, but it is very bad for dogs.

Food Math

Dogs need to be fed the right amount of food for their size. It is as bad to give a dog too *much* food as too *little*. A veterinarian will be able to advise you on the right amount of food for your dog, and will also tell you about the different types of food available.

This Beagle mom is eating alongside her pup.

Even small breeds, such as this adorable Pug, need to be exercised each day off the leash.

Everyday Care

Like humans, dogs need their teeth brushed daily and, especially if they are long-haired, their hair groomed. Owners should also make sure their dog's eyes and ears are clean and examine the **pads** of its feet for cuts or bruises.

After a muddy walk, a dog benefits from a bath or shower, and a rub dry.

Health Care

Dogs will need to visit the veterinarian for regular health checks and if they are ill or injured. The veterinarian will vaccinate your dog to protect it from dangerous diseases.

A veterinarian is **microchipping** this Dogue de Bordeaux puppy.

TRAINING YOUR DOG

All dogs should be taught five basic commands: "Sit," "Down," "Stay," "Come," and "Walk to Heel." They also need to understand the word "No!" A well-trained dog has a happier life, because it is safe to let off the leash.

DOG DATA!

Puppies don't chew to be naughty. It helps them to shed their baby teeth and make room for the adult ones.

Be Consistent

Decide on your command words and stick to them. Don't confuse your dog by saying "Sit!" at first, then changing to "Sit down!" Be consistent and your dog will soon learn what you want it to do. Try not to repeat commands too much or your dog will ignore you.

As well as praising good behavior, you should ignore bad behavior.

The best way to train a dog is to reward good behavior. Give it praise or treats, such as food or play.

Socialization

One important ingredient for producing a happy, confident dog is socialization—getting the dog used to anything it is likely to encounter. Do this from as early an age as possible. Make each new experience fun and be ready with a distraction if the dog becomes nervous. Introduce your dog to people of all ages, other animals, traffic, bicycles, and joggers. In the home, let it become accustomed to everyday noises, such as washing machines and vacuum cleaners.

If it encounters a range of different experiences early on, your dog will be calm in any situation.

GLOSSARY

AKC - American Kennel Club
the organization in the United States that registers pedigree dogs

assistance dog
a dog that is trained to help someone who has a disability with practical tasks

big cat
one of the four members of the cat family that are able to roar—lions, tigers, leopards, and jaguars are all big cats

bobbed
describes a tail that is naturally short. More than eight cat breeds have natural bobtails, and more than 20 dog breeds

booster
a repeat-injection of a mild form of the microbes that cause a serious disease so that a body can maintain natural immunity to the disease

breed standard
the list detailing all the characteristics that a pedigree cat or dog must match before they are registered as pedigree

bull-baiting
a medieval entertainment, where dogs attacked a bull for people's entertainment

camouflage
colors, patterns, or shapes that help something blend into its surroundings

CFA - Cat Fanciers' Association
the world's largest registry of pedigree cats

coursing
chasing prey by sight, rather than by scent

dock
to shorten a dog's tail

domesticated
describes a tame animal that lives alongside humans

double coat
describes the coat of an animal that has two kinds of fur—a thick undercoat and waterproof overcoat

evolve
how a living organism changes very slowly over long periods of time to create new species

FCI - Fédération Cynologique Internationale
the world's largest registry of pedigree dogs

feline leukemia
a blood disease in cats

flush out
to chase an animal out of where it was hiding

leonine
like a lion

mammal
an animal that has a backbone, breathes air, and produces milk to feed its young

microchip
to inject a tiny computer chip into an animal so that it can be identified

mutation
a change in an animal's makeup

muzzle
the area around an animal's nose and mouth

neuter
to remove an animal's reproductive organs so that it is no longer able to breed and produce young

pad
the fleshy part on the bottom of a cat or dog's paw

pecking order
status in a group

GLOSSARY

pit-fighting
the illegal practice of putting two dogs into a pit to fight each other

pointer
a type of dog that will "point" at its prey, allowing hunters to find it

polydactyl
having more than the usual number of toes

sniffer dog
a dog that is trained to use its sense of smell to find things, such as explosives, drugs, or blood

species
a group of animals that share certain characteristics and can breed together to produce young

spray
the action of marking territory with urine by cats or dogs

stop
the slope between the dog's skull and its muzzle

territory
the area that an animal considers its own

toilet training
teaching a young animal, such as a kitten or puppy, to do their business on newspaper or in a dirt box

vaccination
injecting an animal with a mild form of the microbes that cause a serious disease so that its body can build up natural immunity to the disease

vocal
describes an animal or person that makes lots of noise

weaned
describes a baby mammal that has stopped feeding from its mother and has started eating solid food instead of milk

INDEX